"Growth is painful. Change is painful. But nothing is as painful as staying stuck somewhere you don't belong."

-Mandy Hale

The extraORDINARY
Mr. Nobody

A Beginners Guide to Self-Healing

Sekia :)

I always appreciated your energy and your kindness. You're amazing. Stay beautiful.

Love,

Tsanonda Edwards

Cover Design by Steve Gibson of UDIO Edge.

Acknowledgements

Special thanks to friends and family who knowingly and unknowingly witnessed my struggles, accepted them and pushed me to see myself more clearly.

This book is dedicated to those who struggle silently. I hear you….

Table of Contents

"I remember this cat would always come to class with a smile. It was like he never had a bad day..."

-My favorite teacher, **Dr. LaMarr Darnell Shields** *speaking about me as a student at Baltimore City College High School.*

Little did he know the daily agony I went through to maintain that façade...

Don't get me wrong: I know many people have troubled upbringings, and as a kid with my mom and dad in my life, food to eat, clothes on my back and a roof over my head, I had very little to complain about. So, I'm not comparing my life to the thousands of kids I went to school with or the millions of kids that came before and after me.

But my experience is my own, and that makes it different, unique, humbling and one I would like to share and, hopefully, people can learn from.

Because there were mental and emotional obstacles that prohibited my growth into the man I'm still growing into today. What I know to be true is that there are many others whose circumstances make them hide their true selves. Possibly even worse than that, some choose to turn themselves into who they THINK others want them to be...

Now, as a former teacher and current lifelong learner, I've always found a good question useful to provoke thought, so I guess it's only right to kick things off with one: **Have you ever felt like there was nothing about you that made you unique or special?** Or there was nothing that made you stand out from anyone else? If your answer is yes, I'm here to tell you that you aren't alone. From my humble beginnings growing up in inner city Baltimore, Maryland through high school, college and even grad school, I always felt... Plain.

What I mean is, at each and every stop, I've met unbelievable people, and some of them looked kind of like me, or sounded kind of like me, or thought kind of like me. In my mind, they were pretty much just like me. At least that's the way I saw it... With all this 'same-ness,' more often than not, I would think (or over-think) about it and convince myself that me and my contributions were nothing spectacular. For lack of a better word, I felt really ordinary. EXTRA ordinary...

Even with that feeling at the forefront of my thoughts, I believe whole-heartedly that there's one sure thing I've learned: with all the seemingly ordinary 'stuff' we go through as we evolve, **the smallest, miniscule, most irrelevant moment or situation in one person's life could mean EVERYTHING to someone else who's involved.** And because of that, everything and everyone matters. And now, I'll tell you how I came to that simple conclusion. This, ladies and gentlemen, is the story of my life: **The extraORDINARY Mr. Nobody.**

Now, this isn't an autobiography, not in the traditional sense, anyway. I won't spell out the ups and downs of my life in painstaking detail. My personal level of attention isn't set up that way and I'm sure yours isn't either. **The purpose of this book is to give you a little direction in key areas of life that'll help you with choices you'll make in the future and come to terms with choices you've made already.** In fact, my goal is to keep it universal enough to spark your interest with enough detail to paint a vivid picture.

So, some parts will be funny, other parts sad; some parts you'll fully understand, and others may not make much sense. But that pretty much sums up life, right? And it's not just with me; that's with all of us. Our lives seemingly unfold without much rhyme or reason as to why it plays out the way it does. **Other times, much more tragically, we find ourselves playing starring roles in the demise of our own growth...**

More than anything, this book will serve as a beginners' guide to self-healing. How so?

In it, I'll help you understand a few very important parts of my life and, by extension, gain insight on yours. Those important parts? The impact of **school** and religion, the effect **parents** have on their children, coping with the weight of **depression**, preparing for **college or career**, the emotional rollercoaster of raising **children**, and ways to create positive, nurturing **relationships**.

"And exactly how does examining YOUR life help ME, Tsanonda?"

I'm glad you asked! I'm volunteering to be your personal test dummy: I agree to be open and honest about some very personal barriers I worked to overcome. And I'll do that willingly if you to do two things: (1.) think about how you've handled situations in the past and then (2.) mentally work through ways you (or I) could've handled things better.

To assist with that process, at the end of each chapter there's a **TAKEAWAY** and an **ACTIVITY**. The *'Takeaway'* section gives you guidance on how to apply what you've read and an explanation of why it's important. Then, the *'Activity'* offers a simple 'to-do' which will give you something that inspires a change in the way you normally do things.

With all that said, welcome to my life. Or better yet, OUR lives… I pray you learn something and enjoy!

CHAPTER ONE

HIGH SCHOOL and RELIGION Just Don't MIX

Let's start by talking about growing up. We're going to fast forward right past the cute little baby pictures, the dirty diapers, the finger painting, the first steps, the "terrible twos, threes and sometimes fours," etc. While we're at it, let's skip elementary and middle school altogether. I completely understand that those stages of growth are extremely important when attempting to understand and groom your child with regard to their mental and emotional development, blah, blah, blah, blah. But for our purposes, I want to focus on the teen years. That means bypassing the gray area where we're primarily guided by parents and guardians and keying right in on the point where our 'not-so-baby' selves start understanding discipline and making personal decisions for ourselves.

You see, while growing up, there are so many things teenagers have to remember regarding how to act within a given social environment. Many of those rules are based on our personal upbringing and that usually includes our religion.

Whether Christian, Jew, Muslim, Buddhist or any of the other supposed major religions the world over, most people are taught to respect a higher being or power or energy. Along with that worship, we're also given rules to follow as unofficial ambassadors of the religion. Most of us can agree that one of the primary rules we're repeatedly told, and expected to comply with, is simple: **respect others**.

Respect. It's one of the most well-known ideas taught to young people and it generally doesn't discriminate. Respect is the blanket that covers everyone: classmates, teachers, coworkers, elders and pretty much anyone else we come in contact with, whether we know them or not. It even covers objects, as we can count on hearing reminders to respect someone's house, or their car, or even the shoes they're wearing. What I don't recall being taught is exactly how to treat people who chose not to respect me back (not by my parents, anyway).

Back to the point: **religion** combined with **proper upbringing** is important. And I use the word 'proper' loosely because while this idea is universal, most religions view other religions as examples of what NOT to do all the while preaching love and acceptance. Go figure… Anyway, religion and upbringing are often used by parents as the foundation and catalyst for good character in most young people. A tipped-cap bravo to you, Parents!

Now, while you're busy patting yourself on the back for a job well-done, there's an incredibly impactful energy waiting to be unleashed on your children. This monstrous entity? **HIGH SCHOOL.** High school (and sometimes even middle school) works tirelessly to erase all parental forward-thinking and good will.

This 'necessary evil' lasts about four years, Monday through Friday, for at least six and a half hours per day and that doesn't include extracurricular activities. Now, don't get me wrong: **Most parents give unbelievable effort when it comes to molding their children into the perfect representatives of their family.** Children are sent to school with the proper supplies for learning coupled with the hope of doing far better than any family member before them ever has. And then these little darlings have the nerve to be so well-spoken and charming. Just living, breathing perfection! At least most of them try to be…

That said, for the most part, finding a way to fit in becomes the norm for young people. That or trying to stay so far under the radar that people barely notice them. Either way, high school becomes centered around three things (in no particular order and excluding academics): **(1.)** popularity or lack thereof, **(2.)** dealings with the opposite sex and **(3.)** opposition to the 'establishment' (i.e. any teacher, staff member, or even parent/guardian they feel is bent on making their lives miserable). **Yes parents, once high school starts, it's very easy for you to become the enemy** (BUT, take a deep breath, tread lightly and realize that with a lot of patience, understanding and support, no one has to flat line).

Like most students, once I got to high school, I realized that I had a lot to contend with academically and mentally. I also knew that there was one thing that would probably set me apart socially in a big way: **being one of Jehovah's Witnesses.**

Yes, the ones that come to your house on Saturday mornings and attempt, usually in vain, to at least leave you with something spiritual to read. Before I get into my high school reality as one of Jehovah's Witnesses, it's important to dispel some widely accepted, yet not entirely true myths about the religion:

Number 1: *They don't go to anyone's house at 5o'clock in the morning preparing you for anyone's return...* The earliest I've gone knocking on people's doors for 'Field Service' (which is what Jehovah's Witnesses call it) was around 9:00 a.m. and I doubt things have changed much since I've stopped attending, so exaggerations are unnecessary, just like ducking and hiding...

Number 2: *They do believe in Jesus Christ...* For me, that was the most often heard falsehood. Yes, Jehovah's Witnesses believe Jesus is the Son of God, born to Mary and Joseph by means of God's Holy Spirit; manger, three wise men following a star, etc. etc.; all thoroughly believed by Jehovah's Witnesses...

Number 3: *They aren't a random, crazy cult...* Jehovah's Witnesses, as an organization, are God-fearing Christians who have reasons for what they do just like other religions. Some directives that come from the leaders of the organization are different than other religions (for example, the act of 'disfellowshipping' unrepentant believers). That said, it's a religion with rules they expect to be followed regardless of the ripple effects (which are real and lasting, as you'll see)…

Number 4: (Which is true, so I'll call it "Truth 1"): *Jehovah's Witnesses don't celebrate holidays* (including birthdays; I'd never celebrated a birthday until my late teens or early twenties)… All for bible-based reasons, too. Besides being taught that nothing good in the Bible came from celebrating anyone's birthday (King Herod, Pharoah and Job's son's, the only three birthdays mentioned therein, ended with people dying), one of the primary reasons that my mother gave for not celebrating holidays was she didn't want to wait until certain 'societally mandated' times of the year like Christmas or birthdays to celebrate us or give us gifts. In fact, my mother made a point to give my brother and me gifts regularly when she could. This led to my ongoing belief that it's better to acknowledge people and show appreciation for them as often as you can, not just on their birthday. That, while not acceptable to most, makes a lot of sense to me. 'Giving out flowers' early and often is one my favorite mottos to this day…

Now, while I readily admit I owe some of my better qualities and characteristics to growing up as one of Jehovah's Witnesses, (namely, the ability to study, and comprehend important information, my appreciation for the Bible, etc.), being brought up from an early age as one of Jehovah's Witnesses also lead to an extreme turning point in high school and, therefore, my life…

The Turning Point………

Fact: Everyone has at least one turning point in their lives.

A turning point is a point where a vital decision has to be made that has the potential to alter your life for the foreseeable and sometimes unforeseeable future.

Thinking back as an adult, you can clearly see the turning points you've faced. It can be a decision involving career, children, relationships, money, personal or professional investments, narrowing (or even finding) your purpose, etc.; all very important decisions that have potentially life-altering impact. High school is slightly different:

In high school, everything feels like a turning point. Every single decision made as a teenager feels like the biggest decision ever(!) and therefore, what I call a 'faux-turning point:'

When I get my haircut, should I get a part? Turning point. *Should I wear my new sneakers/tennis shoes on Friday or wait until Monday?* Turning point. *Should I catch my regular bus after school OR go ahead and catch the other one? Sure, it'll take me a couple extra hours to get home, but at least I'm riding with my new crush for a few stops, right?* Turning point!

In this particular instance, my first real high school turning point was a legitimate one and one that would affect my life for many years to come. It happened in ninth grade.

Now, upon entering CITY, I focused on participating in class, completing home assignments and classwork, and doing well on tests, quizzes, etc. I also made friends pretty easily; not to mention my brother was a senior so his friends became my 'big brothers and sisters' (shouts to the Class of '94!). That gave me what most would call a decent start to the school year.

It stayed pretty smooth until two things happened: One was my Latin teacher asking me why I couldn't be "more like my brother," as if being me wasn't good enough (this actually started a strong distrust for teachers and accounted for part of my academic slippage… *Most people will admit that a teacher has significantly impacted their lives either positively OR negatively in a way they'll never forget;* and they can usually tell you the teacher, grade, and moment in question; trust me: teachers have a lasting effect on children and it goes well beyond academics). The second thing is what I commonly refer to as 'The Turning Point.'

It came a few weeks into high school during my last period Biology class with Ms. Hill. This particular class was always fun because we had a few class clowns plus our teacher was young and fairly laid back. Even though she was no-nonsense and had high expectations for us,

Ms. Hill also had a sense of humor and, as long as we completed our assignments first, she never had a problem with us laughing and talking to one another quietly. This particular day, we finished our assignment and with a few minutes left in the school day, five or six of us we were laughing about something high schoolers frequently laugh about. Eventually, one young lady, who eventually became one of my closest friends to this day (my sister, Mia J.R.), said: **"Tsanonda, you're funny! But I noticed something: You never curse…"**

As soon as she said that, I felt my heartbeat quicken and it seemed like the room shrunk to at least half its actual size and every eye in the classroom was on me.

Sidebar: Embarrassment is the bane of a young person's existence. Even adults struggle with it; notice how people shut down or, worse yet, explode when embarrassed. Now imagine your head, face, and hands feeling hot or sweaty or both because you sense potential embarrassment as adrenaline surges through your body. Then, on top of that, you see your life flash in front of your eyes, but it's not your past. Instead, it's how you see your life unfolding if you don't respond correctly in this increasingly exasperating situation…

Of course, during this time in a high schooler's life, cursing was a basic rite of passage. Most young people used middle school to hone their 'skills,' so by high school, plenty of kids were pretty fluent. But, as one of Jehovah's Witnesses (a fact none of my classmates knew at that time), I wasn't allowed to curse. Admittedly, that's fairly common across most religions especially with children, but my problem was I had never used a curse word in my life. Not even by mistake or by myself when no one was around just to hear what it would sound like or even when copying a song or movie. I would naturally 'radio-edit' my speech because I couldn't bring myself to curse for fear of some sort of eternal damnation (although Jehovah's Witnesses don't believe people go to hell, or heaven for that matter...).

In fact, to this day, I've never heard my mother, who's still one of Jehovah's Witnesses, utter a single curse word. Never even by mistake or when she didn't know I was listening.

All that said, I was at a very personal, yet very public crossroads: I could honestly and confidently acknowledge Mia's observation, confess to my peers that I was one of Jehovah's Witnesses, and boldly let them know that cursing was one of many things that we didn't do.

OR, I could take door number 2…

"Sh*t, I always curse. F*ck you talking 'bout, girl?"

(I obviously chose the latter…)

Everyone laughed (except Mia, who kind of chuckled and shook her head), the conversation continued, and all was 'right' with the world… I had avoided being embarrassed in school. This feat takes extraordinary skill especially as a Freshman when your peers are experts at making embarrassing moments highlight material for days, months or years to come. And those moments can serve as the social death sentence we sometimes fear.

But, more importantly and most impactful for me, **I had, for the very first time in my life, conformed to peer pressure:** feeling the need to do whatever will gain the acceptance of your friends and associates. When you think about it, it's incredible what a person will do when they're uncomfortable doing it or, worse yet, don't want to do it all…

What amazed me then and now is how quickly the words came out. I put them in the right places and everything. I was weirdly proud of myself. It was the first potentially embarrassing situation I avoided in high school and it allowed me to spend another day with the cool kids. Sadly, it was also the beginning of my life as a conformist and therefore, an amateur actor (or **living liar**).

Now, the lies I told were never intended to be hurtful ones. They were always "I don't want to embarrass myself" lies; the kind that were supposedly harmless and allowed me to appear cool and regular in front of my peers. But, don't get self-righteous on me: it's fairly common to tell lies in order to avoid weird, uncomfortable, or awkward situations or conversations. For example, telling my kids Santa Claus and the Tooth Fairy are real or saying teachers don't have favorites are pretty acceptable 'little white lies' and help days move along more smoothly. Truth be told (pun absolutely intended), my lies did the exact opposite for me and were, therefore, pretty harmful (I mean these are lies we're talking about; no amount of explaining will change that).

The lies took control of my life... I had to keep track of the ones I told, and it became increasingly more difficult to do so. I had to remember why I said couldn't go to someone's birthday party or why a young lady I was interested in couldn't call my house or why "I decided" not to try out for the football team or quit baseball try-outs, all things I desperately wanted to do, but couldn't because my religion wouldn't allow it.

Most people never got to know who I really was, although I tried my best to be a genuinely nice guy. I tried to be considerate and thoughtful and engaging toward everyone I met, but it still felt like I lived two completely different lives. And I couldn't tell anyone about it, so it was mentally, emotionally and spiritually exhausting, even though I didn't realize it at the time. In those moments, I wished I could be what I perceived as normal even if I had to fake it every day. And that's exactly what I did...

TAKEAWAY from CHAPTER ONE

How can you bridge the gap between the expectations religion places on young people and a teenagers' modern reality?

Let's break that down... While religions can be viewed as strict and confusing and overwhelming to young people, the foundation of spiritual experiences should be love: love of self, love of others and love of a Higher Being. So, start bridging that gap by understanding that anything couched in real love can't be all bad. Then, understand that love comes in many forms, so it doesn't always look the same. Prime example for young people: you can love your friends for accepting you, and being open to trying new and exciting things; you can also love your parents for doing what seems like the exact opposite and setting an example of stability and steadfastness by encouraging you to avoid certain things or stay a particular course. It's all love...

Finally, understand that not everyone knows how to love themselves, so loving another person is a process that must be undertaken and learned, just like spirituality. In other words, bridging the gap takes love, understanding, and acceptance. Of self and others...

UNBRIDLED HONESTY: *Being one of Jehovah's Witnesses has made me question my relationship with God and people my entire life... I spoke with a friend (Devonne F.) who I randomly found out also grew up as one of Jehovah's Witnesses. When we briefly talked about it, she captured the Jehovah's Witness experience in a way that almost made me shed tears because of how true and authentic her statement was:*

"Growing up as one of Jehovah's Witnesses makes you feel like you have to be absolutely perfect every single day of your life..."

Just imagine that:

Perfection.

Every. Single. Day.

And if you decide to no longer follow that faith after you've been baptized into it, you'll be disfellowshipped, no longer allowed to associate with or speak to your family or friends.

It's very, very difficult.

And that fear can consume you. Daily...

So, coming to terms with who you are as an individual (specifically spiritually) is vitally important.

ACTIVITY for CHAPTER ONE

Talk to people about their religious and spiritual perspectives. Find out what people's religious views are and what led them to believe the way they do. While you may know a person's religion, why they chose it can be equally as interesting as what they chose. Most importantly, keep an open mind. The reason you ask questions is to learn and gain understanding; not to belittle, judge or condemn.

If religion is too touchy a subject (as it very often is), talk to them about what they do as a career or ask what they value. Some may value having a skill or trade while others may value continuous academic advancement. Ask what they like to do: their hobbies, interests, goals or dreams. These are things that help you understand who a person and, more deeply, how and why they are who they are. Then, turn the figurative mirror on yourself: understanding others can help you define and, sometimes, REfine yourself. But in the end, be your best you. Unflinchingly…

CHAPTER TWO

Why I Hated My Mother

Needless to say, keeping up with this life outside myself was difficult. I wholeheartedly blamed my mother and our religion for every negative situation I encountered. This caused a huge, gaping rift to grow between my mother and me. I resented her for forcing me to be a part of this religion and, in my mind, 'forcing' me to lie to my new friends. I begrudged the fact that I couldn't totally be myself or the 'me' I desperately wanted to be.

It got to a point where I would go to school and have the best time of my life. Laughing, joking and forming bonds that last to this day. And then when the school day was over, I would go home as late as I possibly could and go directly to sleep, usually around 5 or 6pm (if we didn't have a religious meeting to attend). That way I could avoid my mother and the life I felt she created and forced me to conform to.

Following my 'nap,' I'd wake up around the time my mother went to sleep. Then, I'd eat, watch television or play video games, and go back to sleep around 2:00 or 3:00 am and prepare for another day at school. For years, I rarely even did homework. I was able to do well enough on classwork, tests and quizzes, and a few projects and class presentations here and there to pass from grade to grade- though my GPA showed my lack of homework completion.

As for the rift between my mother and me, it grew so wide that **it ended with my mom putting me out of our house February of my Senior Year of high school**. Or did I leave? I'll let you decide…

During that year, I started 'talking' (a term we used as the step before dating) to a young lady I had a crush on since the first day of our freshman year. Yes, you read that correctly: Since the FIRST DAY of our FRESHMAN year in 1993.

*Sidebar: One thing that makes this story interesting is it wasn't supposed to happen. I wasn't supposed to go to CITY. While in Middle School, my grades said, "College Prep," but my mother and our religion said, "Trade School" (because college "promotes greed"). So, my high school choices on paper were Mervo, Carver and another school I can't remember. I do, however, remember my guidance counselor asking me if there was a mistake in my choices. I assured her there wasn't and what she read was what my mother chose. My guidance counselor nodded, then went and changed the choices (based on my grades) to Poly, City and Dunbar (pretty prestigious high schools in Baltimore). **I was actually accepted into Poly**, City's rival school. But my brother, (who transferred from Gilman to CITY in the eleventh grade) told me to transfer to CITY. My mother, surprisingly, allowed me to do so, but she made me go to Poly's freshman orientation to tell them myself I wouldn't be attending their school. After the initial meeting in the auditorium, we went into different classrooms to be* *interviewed. I told the person who interviewed me that I wanted to transfer. His response: "Oh. You do? To CITY?! Are you serious?! Well, have a good life and see you at the Poly/CITY Game. By the way, we're going to beat you!" Ok. CITY FOREVER! (Shouts to the Class of '97!)*

Back to the point: Now, this particular life-changing event started when a friend of ours (Mia again) invited some of us to hangout sometime around Christmas of our senior year. A few guys, a few girls, some food; a simple hangout session. So, we're talking and, as most high school conversations generally go, the topic of relationships comes up. We're talking about couples, break-ups, crushes, etc. and Brandon Wylie (one of my brothers) says, **"Nondie had a crush on Danee'! He even remembers what she had on our first day of school freshman year!"** Everyone, including Danee', looks at me laughing as if to say, "Are you serious?" So, I, at this time never one to disappoint, ran down her entire outfit from head to toe. Everyone including B. Wylie and I laughed hysterically. I'll never forget Danee's response: "You should've said something..."

Sidebar again: How was I able to hang out with friends given my mother and my religion's disdain for 'mixing with the world' (what Jehovah's Witnesses call spending unnecessary time with anyone not a part of the religion), you ask? Well, by this time, I figured out ways to get out of the house. Mainly by relying on my weapon of choice: lying...

I would tell her I was going somewhere with my Jehovah's Witness friends. Then, I would leave the house with those friends and meet up with my classmates. I did this on the regular basis; I even went to Junior Prom without my mother knowing about it until months later when she found the pictures under my mattress. Here's how: my brother, at this time a manager at Checkers, paid for my entire prom (thanks, Gemius!) My 'cousin' Greg (Greg Ash. Love you, Cuz!) picked me up from home after telling my mother we'd be out making extra money cleaning banks after hours. I even asked her to borrow a mop and bucket to make it more believable. Greg then took me to Michael Miller's house (another one of my brothers) to get dressed and he went to go clean the banks while Mike and I went to get our dates and on to the prom. After prom, Mike and I went back to his house, so I could change back into my 'work' clothes. From there, Greg picked me up and dropped me off back home. Planned it down to a science. Albeit a sad one…

Back to the Turning Point: Another thing I won't forget about that hangout session is how Danee's response inadvertently led to the 'Tsanonda versus Mom' situation being recounted now. Here's how…

One evening, I'm upstairs in my room talking to Danee' on the phone. It's February, a couple months after our initial 'I had the BIGGEST crush on you!' encounter. I'm trying to talk in as hushed a tone as possible so that my mother doesn't hear me since talking on the phone with a young lady was a definite no-no in my mother's home.

At some point during our conversation as I'm trying to impress her with my developing wit and intellect, my mother gets on the line from downstairs (these were 'pre-cell phone' days, so we had three cordless phones in the house). She asks if I'm on the phone (no doubt, a rhetorical question) and tells me to get off her phone and she'd better not ever catch us on it again.

The absolute horror...

My biggest concerns flashed in my brain immediately: (1.) What if Danee' decides to never speak to me again? And then, (2.) what if she tells everybody in school what my mother said/did? You all know how I feel about embarrassing situations, right?

So, I decided to take my life into my own hands (figuratively and literally, I guess): I went downstairs to my mother's room and gave her the "I'm 18 years old, can do what I want, and don't ever embarrass me like that again" speech. Her reply? She gave me the "You're not talking to me like that, this is my house and as long as you live here, you'll abide by my rules" response.

Needless to say, **Mable won.**

Long story short, I was packed and gone the next day...

The nerve. I mean, who was she to embarrass me like that? I was a grown man, right? Not only was she not going to embarrass me like that, but who did she think she was? I can make my own decisions, right?

For years I felt like my mother kicked me out of my home… **In my mind, she chose her religious beliefs over her son.** How was it I could work so hard to be approachable and likeable and articulate and caring just to come home to a mother who made it clear that those things were useless and pointless and unimpressive and a waste unless used them to further "Jehovah's kingdom?" I realized years later that it's likely I used that incident to get away from my situation and, therefore, my mother. In my thinking, it was my mother and the religion that she chose for us that caused so much hurt and confusion for me and it impacted my way of thinking, my actions and even my relationships (specifically with women). It all matters…

Since that story didn't end in a quick and awkward reconciliation with me learning my lesson, returning home after accepting Mom's rules and apologizing for my behavior, I have to thank my biological sister Arseendra (I love you dearly, Sis) and B. Wylie and Pops (I love and appreciate you more than you'll ever know, Al Wylie) for giving me a place to lay my head to finish high school and begin college.

Sidebar yet again: B. Wylie pointed out, many years later, that I was homeless for a while. I tried to argue his point because I always had somewhere stay. But, the reality is if you don't have a stable place to consistently stay, you're couch-surfing, you're in between homes, and you don't have a permanent address where you can receive mail or simply rest your head, you are, in effect, homeless.

So, technically, I graduated high school and started college homeless. I'll also admit I can be stubborn, just like my mother...

TAKEAWAY from CHAPTER TWO

What should you do to aid the process of forgiving those you feel have wronged you?

Short answer: You start by forgiving yourself…

You aren't expected to know everything, and that goes for whether you're 17 or 71 years old. While you're accountable for your actions and responsible for your decisions, learning is a process that will literally take forever. So, utilize the present time to be honest about where you've struggled and the barriers you've placed in front of yourself. Then, **take a very deep, controlled breath, and forgive yourself.**

Next, make a habit of empathizing with others (truly looking at arguments, disagreements and the like from someone else's perspective). This can be especially important when working through issues with your parents. If you can understand where they're coming from, that can be the catalyst for a conversation that may well heal your relationship. Now, if you believe the person who hurt you did so maliciously with no basis, rhyme or reason for doing so, then you may have to reevaluate if that relationship is important enough to do the work required to salvage it. **As you can see, I'm not an advocate for simply dissolving relationships.** If any relationship is that easy to let go of, then you should check yourself for being a part of it in the first place…

Now that you've done that, work on forgiving your parents/guardians. When approaching and going through teen years, parents are generally Enemy #1. When I was at that I age I truly believed that my mother hated me… I felt like she woke up to make my life a living hell.

Nevermind, the roof over my head and the food in the refrigerator…

Nevermind, the new clothes, tennis shoes, or video games that she bought for me on the regular basis…

Nevermind, she was a single mother doing the best she could to raise two boys in the Park Heights area of Baltimore…

Now while I don't agree with all my mother's choices for me, I do recognize that she did what she thought was best and I love and appreciate her for being the primary foundation-layer for who I was then and am today. And while I can count on one hand the number of times my mom and I have physically embraced or even said the words to one another, **I love you, Mable. And I know you love me, too…**

ACTIVITY for CHAPTER TWO

Think about your relationship with your parent, guardian, grandmother, grandfather, and/or primary caregiver.

Come to terms with that relationship, whether good or bad. Here's how: If it was a good one, use it as an example of how to be an amazing parent, aunt, uncle, etc. Reflect on those positive memories as you go about even your daily interactions. If it wasn't so good, use it as a catalyst to change your family's legacy. Be the very best, person, parent, auntie, uncle, grandma or grandpa you can be and be a living embodiment of care and consideration for children and others.

Then, as soon as you get an opportunity (**if it's in no way traumatic**), reach out to that person. I'm not saying call with a never-ending stream of tears and go on and on about how much you love them (unless you're so moved, in which case I say go for it!). I do, however, suggest you at least tell them you thought about them even if you don't feel comfortable saying anything else. There is often unimaginable power in what is unspoken… And it really is the thought that counts. Remember, all healing begins with you.

CHAPTER THREE

Product of Divorce and Depression

So far, I've given you a snapshot of my life with Mable and I believe that it's equally important for me to give you some insight on my father: the handsome, funny, hard-working, Army Veteran, **Harry James Edwards.**

Let's start with a kid's eye-view of Mable and Harry's relationship: My mother is from South Carolina and my father is from North Carolina. They met and married after moving to Baltimore and working together at a coat company. After X amount of years of marriage (I still don't know how many…), they must have divorced sometime during my early years as my memory of the actual divorce is nonexistent.

I remember our family living together on Park Heights Terrace and then, having missed or mentally blocked out the divorce/transition period, I remember moving one night to Cold Spring Lane and Reisterstown Road with just my mother and brother. Then, my dad started picking my brother and I up to spend time with him, my sister and my step mother (Hey, Mary!) usually every other weekend or so in East Baltimore. It's interesting the things you suppress, or the things hidden from young people. A **whole divorce. I don't remember any of it**…

What's funny (or maybe sad) about it is there are two things I remember most about growing up following the divorce (1.) eating government-issued food and (2.) shopping at the Thrift Store for my clothes.

Sidebar: One thing about Welfare food that sticks with me to this day is that damn powdered milk… It's the worst stuff I've ever tasted in my life. To this day, I don't drink or use milk below 1%. I hope that non-milk, just add water, powder to liquid substance has been wiped off the planet. No one deserves that…

Back to the point: I tend to believe my mother and father's divorce led to many significant household changes. The most obvious change was financial and with no father in the house, it meant less income. That doesn't mean my mother didn't work hard and do what she could, or my dad didn't take care of us, because he did. It just meant one household income and when Mom is unemployed, life was more difficult.

The most obvious example I can give to show the difference in my life financially is purchasing sneakers. I remember when my mother bought them for us, she had to get them from Payless. There was one on the corner of Reisterstown Road and West Cold Spring Lane for a while. So, I would have all black "Coasters" that she bought from there. After a couple months when it was my dad's turn to buy shoes for school, we would have shoes like Jordans (my first pair was a pair of Air Jordan 3's) or Lotto's (with the multi-colored Velcro signs). That's a pretty big difference.

Mom and Dad's separation also led to Saturday shopping trips to the Thrift Store (or Goodwill). I remember loving the Thrift Store. The toy section was always the best part for me. Hundreds of donated toys placed near television sets, cameras and hundreds of books. My brother and I would busy ourselves playing with the toys or reading books while my mother looked through all the different racks for clothes we could wear. I never really noticed labels on clothing until I wore a shirt my mother bought me from the Thrift Store to school...

At this time, my brother and I were attending Gilman, a private school in West Baltimore (again, Dad kept providing). One day, I wore a shirt to school that had a small, aqua-colored "Brunswick Bowling" logo stitched on the front. One of my classmates innocently asked about it: "Do you bowl for a team?" I was puzzled at first, but he pointed to my shirt and asked again. I muttered no, mentioned my father bowled for a league (which was true) and quickly changed the subject. Needless to say, that was the last time I wore that shirt, at least without a sweater covering it.

That was the day I became acutely aware of the differences between myself and the kids I went to school with. **My classmates had the last names of judges, lawyers, doctors and famous painters** ('paintings hanging in national museums' type of famous painters) and I was a poor kid from the inner city who had to catch public transportation to school, since my mom didn't have a car. Still, I worked hard and held my own academically. Interestingly, after my first two years in private school, I transferred to Greenspring Middle School for eighth-grade (shout out to Toy, Kilo, Lakesha, Jacob and all other Greenspring folk!) and graduated as the male valedictorian of my class. Was it through an outstanding work ethic or maybe an extreme determination to excel in class? Not quite...

Simply put, what I was taught in eighth grade at Greenspring I had already learned in sixth grade at Gilman. It was like a yearlong review of information I learned two years prior. Let me repeat that: **Two. Years. Prior.** And don't get me wrong: my eighth-grade class had incredibly intelligent students, just as many public schools across Baltimore did and do. But that doesn't negate the fact that the education we were given wasn't the best. You do the math...

Sidebar: The best example I can think of to show the contrast between private and public education was my ongoing struggle to learn the states and their capitals. It was called "The Bag Test" or something equally clever and horrifying. So, my Geography teacher gave everyone a blank map of The United States. After placing certain states in a brown paper bag, each student had to pull one state out. We would then complete three tasks for the state we selected: find it on our map, label it with its capital, and then label each bordering state with the states and their capitals. And our teacher was sure not to include states with less than four or five bordering states. The stress was so overwhelming for me I had to take the test three or four times before I passed it. Fast forward to

8th grade in public school: Our test asked us to list each state and capital alphabetically the same way we learned it in class. That's a pretty big difference.

Back to my father: I'll never forget the time my father called my brother and I to personally tell us we couldn't go to Gilman anymore because he could no longer afford it. **I'll also never forget how angry he got with us.** Why? Well, my father valued a good education and my brother and me were excited while hearing the news. We no longer wanted to be in private school anyway. The education was second to none, and my friends were amazing (shouts to Bentley, J.V., Sykes, Tony, Ike, Kenny, etc.!), but I think we both wanted to learn and socialize in an environment with more people that looked like us (read: Black). Sadly, and strangely ironic? My brother and I were celebrating not having to go back to private school and my father couldn't bear not being able to afford that same private school education... Perspective is so interesting; one situation viewed entirely different ways. And that led to the next Turning Point in my life.

It's an extremely intimate look at my Dad and, for reasons that will soon be obvious, we won't call it the beginning, but rather the end:

My father committed suicide…

He killed himself when I was about twelve years old.

Pointed a gun to his heart and pulled the trigger.

In his mind, I'm sure he thought he failed me, my brother and our sister because he wasn't able to provide for us the way he wanted to, although to us, we had any and everything we could ask for; he made sure of it. I guess we were too young to understand the strain it put on him to provide all he did for us especially a superior education. He was the best father in the entire world, at least in my eyes...

There were other factors I came to know of later that added to my father's self-inflicted demise (when family members figured I could handle it better, I guess; and I still don't know how much of its true), but for a long time, I blamed myself... Since then, one of the theories I've come to on my own and accepted is him not feeling like enough of a man to continue with life. **Essentially, he felt he needed to leave this wonderfully horrible place called earth**.

It wasn't until about 25 years after his death I learned my father was diagnosed with Bipolar Disorder/Manic Depression. That type of information is important for families to be aware of and dissect as it affects peoples' lives on so many levels. I think often about just how different my life would have been if my father was around during high school and as I grew into a man. More importantly, it was essential for him to know what he was facing so he could receive the necessary help, support and encouragement.

INTERLUDE: Train up a child in the way he should go…

Depression is a very serious, very draining, often painful illness. It can make your head, heart and, at times, your body ache exhaustingly. It can make you do and think things that can be destructive mentally and physically. Though I was never formally diagnosed with depression, I would go into what research told me were depression-induced 'caves,' where I would stay locked in my room or, once I got older, my apartment for days at a time; I wouldn't eat; I wouldn't answer phone calls; I wouldn't bathe… I don't remember how often during the course of a year it would happen, but I know that I would need these times to recharge. In those times, I felt the need to disappear into myself.

Sidebar: I do recall the month of November being a difficult month for me. It's the month I associate with making a decision that continues to have far-reaching consequences. While I won't go into specifics about it, I'll say that some decisions aren't meant to be made by young people without support. Equally, or possibly more importantly, the actions that young people engage in that lead to adult-like decisions can have devastating effects. That's why it's vitally important to engage young people in ongoing dialogue about their relationships, their course of thinking, and what they're doing. Being a good listener and true advocate of young people can make an incredible difference with regard to their thought process and, therefore, the decisions they make. Understand that a young person's way of thinking can ultimately have mental and physical implications that haunt them well into adulthood. It all matters.

Back to it: So, this need to recharge myself stemmed from a feeling of unrelenting pressure: pressure to be the funny guy or the smart guy or the fake-dumb/silly guy or the compassionate guy or the 'whatever I felt was necessary' guy almost on command. I was always prepared to be what I thought people wanted or needed at the time they wanted or needed it.

And while all of these 'personalities' were a part of me, I found myself juggling them like I was in a never ending one-man play assuming the role of all the characters. And that's why it wasn't really on command.

No one forced or even asked me to be a certain way. Instead, I reasoned, it's easier to be everything people wanted me to be as opposed to defining myself, even if that definition was still 'yet to be determined,' as I was finding and designing myself (which happens to be ok). Instead, I placed myself in positions to be a walking, talking puppet, bending to understand and fulfill everyone else's desires. And in hind sight, although it made me hate my life sometimes, it worked: Everyone loved this me that wasn't really me…

A Depression Full Disclosure: Have I thought about taking my life? Short answer: Yes… But I now realize there's so much to live for: sons, a wife, friends and family who need and love me and I need and love in return. And I'm having so much fun rediscovering my purpose. Too much life to live and stories to create. Plus, I have to believe the world would be much less amazing without me (this isn't ego talking; those who suffer from depression need to know how needed we are. Even if that means reminding ourselves…).

TAKEAWAY from CHAPTER THREE

How does one navigate and cope with the initial and lasting effects of mental trauma and the decisions leading to it?

Takeaway 1: Divorce/separation has a long-lasting effect on everyone involved. If one or both are options in your relationship, make sure you're considerate of those who are affected. Yes, the decision is yours and you'll imminently have to live with it, but others have to live with it as well and that front row seat can be almost or equally as painful. The ripple effects of your decisions are lasting. Understand the impact on you and others and work to make the best decisions possible, for you, and those who have the pleasure of sharing your life.

Takeaway 2: Depression is real…

It's heavy and lonely and difficult to bounce back from. As a 'son of suicide' (following my dad's death), I know there are times when people want to give up and see suicide as the only viable option. And with that history in my family, it means I have to be acutely aware of my feelings and any triggers that lead to darker thoughts. I also have to be aware of what I call **'reverse triggers'**: things that pull me out of dark places and give me the energy and motivation to press on in this beautiful mess called life.

ACTIVITY for CHAPTER THREE

Take a few minutes to list the 'NOUNS' (the people, the places, the things) that make you happy or make you feel better about yourself. My 'reverse-triggers' are books, movies, friends and prayer.

When you start feeling down or sadness starts to creep in, reach out to those people, visit those places, or come in contact with those things. It might help you feel better.

If you're really feeling down, reach out to a professional who can offer guidance and assistance (therapists are amazing!).

For immediate help, call 1-800-273-8255 or text GO to 741741

*****Special shout out to those who can sense a shift in someone's energy, make the effort to check in on those who battle depression, and offer quick words of encouragement or a hug. Trust me: it doesn't always seem like it, but it's appreciated...*****

CHAPTER FOUR

COLLEGE

Part I: How Doing Wrong Set Me Right

After many adventures, stories, learning experiences and friends unlimited, high school eventually had to come to an end. At CITY, a requirement for graduation was applying to at least one college, regardless of our plans after high school. So, applied I did; anything to keep the teachers and counselors off my back.

The problem was, I was a straight C+ student. This, coupled with my easy-going and teacher-friendly demeanor, gave me the perfect balance necessary to be an average student headed toward graduation and a leap into the work force as a postal worker or fire fighter or some other outstanding, yet college-not-necessary career.

So, to fulfill those graduation requirements, I applied to two colleges: Coppin State College (now Coppin University) and Morgan State University (MSU). Then, a funny thing happened on the way to graduation: I was accepted at both. I was completely and utterly shocked. How does an average student get into a university? Apparently, a pretty decent SAT score will do that for you. So, in I was: Morgan State University, here I come.

College started the way high school ended for me and I don't mean that in the best way... My first day on campus, I had to take a placement test I'm sure I could have done well on, but Mia (yes, that Mia again!), who was the real kind of intelligent and not the fake, lazy, unfocused kind like yours truly, finished the test before me. So, instead of waving good-bye and finishing the test, I decided I wasn't planning on being left behind by the only person I knew up to that point, and I left before finishing the test. So, my first order of business was developmental courses (the classes you take in college when the university believes you're not quite ready for college level math and/or reading).

Then, to add insult to injury, I forgot Morgan was affectionately known as CITY's **'13th grade.'** Why 13th grade, you ask? Because so many people from CITY go to Morgan that it's like high school all over again. The problem? When you're paying for your education, a constant focus on making friends and partying isn't the wisest course of action, and that's exactly the route I chose...

I already had friends, met new ones easy, and didn't push myself to excel in the classroom, even after being placed on academic probation following an emergency appendectomy in November and spending most of my first semester at home on bed rest. I returned to school and spent my second semester partying and trying to meet as many people as possible. Same for the third semester. Then, another funny thing happened on my way to my fourth semester in college: **I was kicked out of school** (Turning point…)

Apparently, one too many times on academic probation and my so-called 'gift of gab' failed me: Morgan State and its Admissions Department didn't accept the Academic Appeal statement I so expertly crafted. (special shouts to my first college mentor, Lonnie Morris, for trying to keep me focused!) So, out into the cold harsh world of work I went.

It's funny how seemingly disastrous obstacles become the calling you ignored. Amen…

Kicked out of College- INTERLUDE One: Practicing My Purpose…

I ended up leaving MSU with quite a few people, including myself, doubting I'd ever be back.

The reality: Chances of a black man graduating from college are slim since jail, or death by homicide is the usual trajectory. But, a black male failing out of school? **Avoid being one statistic and become another one: a drop-out.** And I was perpetuating that very stereotype. But I didn't want that to be the period on the end of life's sentence for me. As cliché as it may sound, I knew I had more to offer Morgan, the world and myself. So, I decided on another route:

AmeriCorp…

The first thing I had to do was figure out a way to make money and get back into school. I knew getting a job wouldn't be difficult, and I didn't have much choice since I was primarily taking care of myself and back home with my mother (that emergency appendectomy episode had me literally pleading at her front door to let me back in; which she did after taking me to the hospital). The difficulty was the thought of saving enough money to get back into school. **Funny how a few years prior, I thought college wasn't for me and now I was dedicating myself to making it back.**

I figured it would take at least a year to save the money I needed. That amount of time was upsetting because, after maturing a little and gaining some perspective, I knew that by the time I got back into school, life would have changed so much. My friends would have graduated, transferred or dropped out themselves. So, my goal was three-fold: Get back into school, do so as quickly as possible, and do whatever it took to stay there.

It really took some soul-searching and prayer, since it was one of the first times in my life I had to admit and accept defeat, more importantly, at my own hands. It was paramount to, well, suicide…

I lived my college life absurdly recklessly and, reaping what I had sown, I got nothing. And the worst part was that I had no one to blame but myself. So, I started applying for jobs at different malls and even grabbed an Employment Guide from a newsstand thinking the more options the better. Sure enough, I saw an advertisement that would change my life forever.

It was an advertisement to join AmeriCorp, an organization launched by President Bill Clinton. Its purpose was to "meet the nation's critical needs in education, public safety, health, and the environment." AmeriCorp was all about community service and made my return to Morgan more tangible by adding two incentives that made my job hunt and college readmission an instant possibility: they offered a bi-weekly stipend and $3,000 toward college. So, I applied, interviewed and was accepted. Amen.

After working for eight months in an after school and summer program at an elementary school in Southwest Baltimore (huge thank you to my James McHenry family: Monte', Tim Christmas, Kellie, Regina, Jennifer, Renee', Erica and Tony!), I was accepted back in school. Plus, I learned that educating people was part of my purpose. You couldn't pay me to believe I didn't have God's favor!

Esteem Boost- INTERLUDE Two:

I finally made it back into Morgan. Shortly after returning, one of the greatest things that could happen to someone that struggled with finding himself and had issues with self-esteem, while pretending the very opposite, happened. Went something like this…

One day, I'm walking into Holmes Hall (the building that English Majors use for classes) around 8:00 am. I can't remember why I was on campus so early (I'm more of an 'after 10:00 am' type of student/person), but I ran into one of my professors, the late Dr. Michael Bayton, leaving out as I was heading in. I said good morning, he said hello and then stopped me to ask how things were going. I told him things were going pretty well in his and a few other classes. He laughed and, after telling me to continue working hard, said something that caught me completely off guard:

"Mr. Edwards: You're a brilliant young man. Don't ever forget that. Enjoy your day."

Then, he walked off. I looked after him in astonishment and finally got out a delayed thank you as he went out the door.

First, no one had ever called me brilliant before. Secondly, it came from Dr. Bayton... This was a man who shook his head from side to side at what he called people's "interesting" responses in class and very sarcastically, yet hilariously wished them "luck in life" on a regular basis. I assume a large part of it was how well I did in his and other classes, especially once I got into my major courses (English). Following my 'drop-out' scare, I definitely developed a renewed focus on my studies.

Sidebar: Strangely, this is yet another thing I owe to my mother raising me as one of Jehovah's Witnesses: Starting when we were really young, my brother and I spent hours on Sundays reading chapter after chapter after chapter of the Bible, explaining to my mother what we read and "making "practical application" to present life... Dr. Bayton was an English Professor and comprehension was my forte'. So, reading and understanding 'strange,' long text like Pride and Prejudice or Ethan Frome or anything Shakespeare wasn't that much different from doing the same thing with Bible writers like King David, King Solomon or The Apostle Paul. Add to that the fact that my brother and I couldn't go outside to play until we finished with our Bible studies and you get a set of fairly quick learning young men. So, while we didn't like it, it gave us the ability to read quickly with understanding and explain overall and subtle messages in text. In other words, it was like college…

Sidebar 2: And that reminds me of yet another defining moment in college. I arrived for one of my Shakespeare class late (as was my norm in college unless specifically forbidden by a professor) and I was stopped by a friend in the hallway. He told me not to go into the classroom because another student was trying to start a petition against me and/ or my professor. I was told the petition said that our professor (Dr. Sheffey) showed me favoritism because there was no way I could have passed the midterm exam... You see, my brother (Larry Saddler) and I were running really late for the midterm. Once we got to class, Dr. Sheffey said there was probably no point in taking it, because we were so late and had so little time. I quickly pleaded our case, figuring that any grade we earned was better than a 0% for not taking it. Long story short, we took the test and I got either an A or a really high B. I figure the person that started the petition believed there was no way I could've done that without cheating or being given a boost in my grade by my professor. There was no way I was intelligent enough to pull that off. There was no way me and my friends would consistently use Loyola's library to study until 2am most nights. To him, I was "less than…" That moment made me think of many times I felt people thought I wasn't good enough. Although, to my knowledge, nothing ever came of the petition, there was a time when that would've negatively impacted my outlook, but at that time, it was fuel to do even better. And if he's reading this, God bless you, Brother.

Back to the point: Needless to say, I'll never forget Dr. Bayton's words (Rest well, Doc). Whether he was exaggerating or not, it was exactly what I needed to hear, because I started a streak of four or five consecutive semesters with a GPA above 3.5 and after being kicked out of school years before for poor grades, I graduated Morgan with a 3.0 cumulative GPA and a one Semester stint on the Dean's List with a perfect 4.0 GPA. Thank God for Loyola's library, Stokos chicken and all those who took that academic ride with me. #MorganMade

College- Part II: The Cost

"Don't ever take out school loans."

-Author Unknown…

That's a direct quote from plenty of individuals as soon I told them I was going to college. The conversation would generally go as follows:

Person: "Hey, Tsanonda! What's up?"

Me: "Maintaining and getting ready for college!"

Person: "Congrats, man! You got any scholarships?"

Me: "Nope."

Person: "Oh, ok. How about grants?"

Me: "Naw…"

Person: "Well, my only advice: DON'T TAKE OUT SCHOOL LOANS!"

Me: "Ok. Understood!"

(What do you think I did?)

Fast forward eight years and over $100,000 in undergraduate and graduate school loans later, things started looking pretty bleak. I was eventually told, while attending school, that loans aren't that bad. You just have to "stay on top of them" and whatever you do, "never go into default!"

(What do you think I did?)

I can tell you what I didn't do: I didn't stay on top of it and, instead, went into default. Innocently of course, if there's such a thing. I actually 'misremembered' that I had up to six months following graduation from graduate school to notify the federal government of my financial situation and begin making payment arrangements (my understanding was I had a year). I was applying for doctoral studies at Morgan State's Urban Educational Leadership Program a year after graduating from the University of Baltimore with my master's degree in Human Services (big shouts to Dr. Pearson, Dr. Hudgins and the Human Services family at UB and Coppin!) when I was denied Financial Aid due to my default status. While paying back those loans is still a work in progress, the moral of that story is stay on top of all financial situations as it may cost you that house, that business, or that degree…

All that said, two things made the cost of (or **investment in**) college totally worth it: First, my ever-expanding network of friends (Shout out to all Morgan State University Alumni, especially my fellow English Majors, and those who shaped me in the Office of Community Service: Tish, Reggie, Mothyna, Munir, Shug, Anjy, West, Faith, Steph, Carney, KimGreen, Larry C., Larry S., etc.) and, secondly and more importantly, helping me come to a better understanding of the greatness within me.

Now, onto ways to make college work without signing your life away…

First and foremost, parents, if your child is still in your home and under your care you will have to fill out a FAFSA for her/him. Trust me, I understand the "those college folk don't need to know my business, and I'm not filling out those online forms" mentality. We must get over that… There's literally NO OTHER WAY for your child to get into school. And I've personally seen so many young people with tremendous academic potential miss out on college because their parents refused to fill out this information. Besides, **filling out those FAFSA forms opens the door for grants and scholarships (free money!) for your child.** This is one of those times it's important to think more of them and less of you.

Now, kiddos; your job is simple: get the very best grades you can throughout your middle and high school matriculation. Whether you feel college is an option for you or not, work to get the very best grades you possibly can and throw in some extracurricular activities as well. This shows, not only your ability to handle progressively more difficult work, but it also shows consistency and your capacity to work with others. **Consistency, positive progression, and the ability to work with others are characteristics you'll need in most if not all situations life sends your way.** College, career, relationships, anything... Add to that the ability to follow directions, a pleasant attitude, and a sense of humor and you're in a great position to excel.

So, what if you get accepted into college and you weren't offered any scholarships or grants? My advice? Skip the four-year college treatment. Just for now, though. Do this instead:

Head to a community college for two years and then transfer your credits into a four-year college or university. This does a few things for you. First, it gives you the opportunity to continue sharpening your skills as a student in a much more intimate setting since community colleges are much smaller than most four-year universities. While you won't be able to stay on campus at most community colleges, you still get college experience with a diverse group of students without being thrown into the deep end of the 'college pool.' Secondly, you complete your courses and you graduate with an AA (Associates of Arts) degree to put on your resume. Community college courses are similar to those at a four-year college and completing those courses adequately will show that positive progression and consistency I mentioned. Lastly, and most importantly given the financial make-up of this conversation, community college costs three times less than a traditional four-year university. Repeat: **THREE. TIMES. LESS. And some community colleges are opening their doors to students for FREE!**

Yes, you can lessen the cost of a four-year college by commuting back and forth (which subtracts room and board and a meal plan from your expenses), but the reality is you don't have those non-class expenses at a community college plus the cost of classes alone at a community college is approximately half what it is at a four-year college or university. Half of anything is a big deal, especially when you're talking about thousands and even tens of thousands of dollars.

So again, if furthering your education is your choice, DO IT! Just do it wisely...

TAKEAWAY from CHAPTER FOUR

Does furthering your education have a long-lasting impact on your life in the present and how does it affect the life you create for yourself in the future?

Truth 1: College is not for everybody.

Everyone is not built to pay, go into debt for or make the best of a college education and atmosphere. Some folks just aren't that interested in attending more school. And if you're sure that you fall into that category that's fine, too. Which leads me to truth two…

Truth 2: Everyone still must learn.

Whether in school, college, on the job, when starting a business or entering the military, you still have more to learn… It's called "training."

Don't trick yourself into thinking that if you don't go to college you'll never need to take another class or learn anything for the rest of your life. There's always a need to gain additional knowledge regardless of your chosen life track. College happens to be viable and valuable option, if executed well.

ACTIVITY for CHAPTER FOUR

Write down three long-term goals and three short-term goals for each long term one. Your long-term goals should come first because your short-term goals should help you achieve your long-term ones. For instance, one of my long-term goals was completing this book, so a few short-term goals were to brainstorm what the chapters would be about, form an outline, then commit to writing.

FOR YOUNG PEOPLE SPECIFICALLY: At least one of your long-term goals should include your choice of college, career and/or entrepreneurial endeavor. While you're not expected to know exactly how your life will play out at a young age, it's better to plot a path and change direction than to have no direction at all. One of the worst things you can do is choose to let life unravel on its own.

You're the author of your story. It's up to YOU to make it a best seller…

CHAPTER FIVE

The Day My Son Died...

"Thank you for choosing the Johns Hopkins Radiology Department..."

That's what the card I received in the mail from Johns Hopkins said. It was followed by a statement about the care that was provided and an announcement of a survey to follow in the coming weeks. I have yet to receive that survey...

About five years after college, I was blessed with a baby boy we named Kai Tsanonda. About eight months after he was born, Kai, his mom, and I went into the hospital on Friday, August 5th, 2011 because he had to have an MRI. One side of his tongue was larger than the other and he had a very slight stillness or sag on the right side of his face/lip which signaled possible nerve damage doctors were slightly concerned about. While they didn't believe that anything was terribly wrong, they wanted to get an MRI to make sure. And that's the beginning of my problem with doctors...

Don't get me wrong: I'm a firm believer that the general health of humanity must have a steward. Some of my fondest memories are of doctors giving me a cast after breaking my wrist in 4th grade, getting stitches after putting a knife through my hand in middle school and finally the countdown that led to being put to sleep for that emergency appendectomy during my freshman year of college. So yes, doctors can be pretty ok. Sometimes...

Because there's always the flip side of the coin. Like the time doctors were told my 'Uncle John' was allergic to penicillin. They "forgot," gave it to him anyway, and he passed... Then, there's the time my mother called me from her job and told me the right side of her body felt numb. As soon as she told me, I remembered reading somewhere that the numbness she mentioned was sometimes a sign of stroke, so I told her we needed to get her to the hospital immediately. Apparently, the folks at the hospital missed that day in class, because after she relayed her symptoms to the staff at the Emergency Room, she was sent home to get rest. She had five more strokes that day and is currently disabled with little to no use of her dominant hand...

Back to Kai... Needless to say, when doctors said my son had to have an MRI, the first question that came to mind was how can you possibly get an infant to stay still long enough? Even adults are told multiple times to be still inside the machine. Their answer:

They would have to sedate him...

Realizing our instant concern, doctors assured us it would take about a month before they could perform the procedure because they'd first have to get a team of specialists to ensure the correct dosage of the inhaled sedative and verify all precautions necessary for a patient his age and weight. After assuring us all details were finalized, and the risk was extremely minimal, his appointment was set for 8:30 a.m. that Friday morning in August.

Everything was set and ready to go. We arrived early to ensure things would go as smoothly as possible and to settle ourselves. Most importantly, we wanted to make sure Kai was ok, or as ok as could be expected when leaving your eight-month old in the hands of strangers, albeit professionals. Unbeknownst to his mother and me, the medical team had to make a decision during Kai's procedure that would change our lives forever…

After being given the sedative, he didn't stay sedated (apparently after months of research by their experts, they couldn't configure the correct dosage). So, they administered a second dose….

During this time, his mother and I had gone to get something to eat and got back to the children's area of the hospital around 9:10 am, five minutes before the little one was due to be finished. 9:10 turned to 9:15 and 9:15 turned to 9:16… Instantly, 'mother's intuition' kicked in and his mom went to the front desk to see what the hold-up was. The receptionist said "He should be finished shortly. Have a seat and the doctor will be out soon."

After a couple minutes, back to the receptionist's desk… "Ok. Have a seat and let me give them a call. The doctor will be out shortly." Another couple minutes, back to the receptionist's desk. "I'll call the doctor again right now." This time, Kai's mom refused to leave the front desk.

The receptionist told the staff that we were growing increasingly impatient, so a nurse came out and asked us to follow her into a room in the back. I remember the nurse reminded me of a young Mrs. Claus. She was sweet and endearing and literally looked like a young Mrs. Claus. She sat us down and asked how we came up with Kai's name. We told her how much he loved water, which happens to be what his name means. She told us about being from North Carolina and how she recently moved to Baltimore with her husband. We asked about the part of North Carolina she was from and told her parts of both our families lived "down south." It was an incredibly light and soothing conversation. Given what would happen less than five minutes from then, **I completely understand the reason for it and I appreciate that nurse's efforts...**

While we were sitting there, in walks the doctor/anesthesiologist and a medical student. I remember four things happening that made it one of the most memorable moments in my life (**and yet another turning point**):

1.) the doctor having a seat to compose herself,

2.) the look of absolute terror on the accompanying med student's face (that she desperately tried to mask),

3.) the way the doctor licked her lips every few words,

and finally,

4.) the words: "he coded…"

"Coded…"

That was doctor talk for "Your son died."

That moment instantly put so much into perspective for me: the importance of appreciating every moment you can, never allowing people to affect me so much that I lose sight of what's most important, and, finally, making time to show people how much I love and/or appreciate them.

After the anesthesiologist explained what happened including the fact that Kai was resuscitated (by a code team that we heard being called while we ate, but thought nothing of it), we were shown into the back where the procedure had taken place and it was, by far, the most eerie feeling in the world. I had never experienced complete silence in a hospital until now. Adding to the silence were the looks on the faces of all the nurses and doctors on the unit that made it even more stifling: Each and every eye was on us with looks of concern and sadness, some tears, and, I guess, compassion…

When Kai looked up and recognized us, he reached out for us so quickly and smiled his crooked smile. His mom grabbed him and couldn't contain her emotion. She held him for what seemed like hours and I let her. She needed that... She then gave him to me and I held him and looked at him; stared at him really. His eyes were dilated, and the nurse said he seemed much calmer now that we were there. Was that a happy ending? Absolutely! And he's one of the most amazing kids in the world. Issues and all...

So, what made this uber-emotional situation so profound for me?

Truth: There was a time that I was angry about having a child. Yes, angry...

I had plans for myself and envisioned my life playing out a certain way. I remember when I was a teacher and parents and colleagues would sometimes say: "Mr. Edwards. You're pretty incredible with children! What's your secret?"

Humbled, my response was usually the same: "I adore children. Absolutely love them! The best part: I give them back at dismissal!"

So, having my son at 30 years old made me feel like the passion and effort I committed to building myself and my personal dreams would now be poured into raising a child.

No more writing a book…

No more doctorate…

No more life as I knew it…

And that made me angry. A good father, yes. But, angry…

And then, that day in the hospital, I heard a whisper:

"Are you sure you don't want him? Because he CAN be taken…"

That moment changed my life because I figured out why people run from responsibility and blame the gifts God gives in the form of our children. The reality is this: children don't stop dreams. We stop dreams… Children don't impede progress. We impede progress… Children don't deter greatness. We deter greatness…

You want proof?

You're reading the book I supposedly couldn't finish…

Kai's Mom is now "Dr. Kai's Mom…"

And life, while definitely not as I knew it, is even better…

So, stop being selfish and give these babies everything you can. The bottom line is there's no excuse for not taking care of your children. The least you can give is your time. More importantly: **There are countless people who would give any and everything to see their child(ren) one more time or to even have a child… So NEVER take yours for granted.** Amen.

TAKEAWAY from CHAPTER FIVE

Do your choices REALLY matter or is resilience and bouncing back from those choices more important?

First, understand that death is a fate that will befall us all. We should cherish and value our lives because we **only get one**. Make the most of it. Avoid choices that will make your stay on this planet a short one. **And choose your circle of friends and associates wisely.** There's probably no choice more important than that. It's sad when people you choose to be around don't value their lives OR yours…

In addition, those choices are just that: YOURS. Make the best ones you can because you'll have to live with them and whatever positive or negative they bring. Don't blame others for the choices you make and when you make a mistake, pick yourself up and set your course right. The key to mistake-making and navigating bad choices is to make them your enemy. It's not that you'll never make a mistake, because you will, but it's so much easier to learn from the paths of others. Pay attention to their successes and heed their failures as well. That way you don't make the mistakes others have. Feel free to put your personal touch on the way you do things, but don't make the same mistakes others make for no better reason than you wanted to try it yourself. Be better than that, because you are…

ACTIVITY for CHAPTER FIVE

Take the time to love on yourself and your loved ones. Go give hugs, make jokes and spend time. Right now.

GO!

****

You back?! Good!

Now, because life is so short, in our quest to create moments, we're not always as focused in the moments that matter and the moments that ARE. It's called "mindfulness." Mindfulness is being aware of your mind, body and feelings in the present moment in an attempt to create calm.

Now, try it: through meditation or yoga or prayer or just being still… Mindfulness absolutely matters. As does self-care.

****

Now, write down the names of your closest friends, then the names of your most avid supporters, then the names of your role models and, finally, the names of your mentors.

Next, beside, under, or near those names, write down what these special people add to your life. Once you've done that, find a way to show how thankful you are for what they add to your life. Write a note, type an email, send a text, make a phone call, or meet up for lunch. Find a way to show genuine appreciation.

As for those you gave these sacred titles to and, upon reflection, they don't add to your life, take a deep breath, and figure out how to shift that dynamic.

No, I won't say, "drop them immediately." **Remember, people deserve second chances and opportunities for redemption.** Give them a chance to be the addition to your life that you (hopefully) are to theirs. If that doesn't work? Drop them immediately...

After you get through that self-examination and reflection, do yourself these three favors:

1.) Acquire life insurance

2.) Create a will

3.) Research and think about pre-arrangement services (shout out to Wylie Funeral Home for offering this service @ wyliefh.com)

Trust me: You need these things. While death is generally uncomfortable to think about, it's important to be mindful of inevitable life situations before it's too late. And that means securing your end of life transition before your life transitions...

CHAPTER SIX

ALL Relationships are Important (Even the ones that aren't)

RELATIONSHIPS...

One of my absolute favorite topics.

Always of interest, relationships are a key part of anyone's existence and are especially important to me. Friendships, familial relationships, intimate relationships, professional relationships. Regardless of their nature, all relationships have their fair share of rewards and challenges. The best part? Once you're able to navigate the ups and downs of most relationships, unbelievably solid bonds can be created; ones that can last a lifetime.

Now, because I realize that intimate relationships are usually of utmost interest to most people, let's begin there.

First, I'll start with an 'Intimate Relationship Math Problem':

SLANDER + LIBEL = LAWSUIT

Slander (noun): a false and defamatory oral statement about a person

+

Libel (noun): a statement published without just cause and tending to expose another to public contempt

=

Lawsuit (noun): a case before a court.

Needless to say, all names, people and places will remain confidential in order to protect the identities of those involved and, most importantly, to avoid retaliatory measures.

I'm kidding! But, I'm not…

Truth be told, there's no reason to put names or endless stories of my relationships gone right or wrong. There's equally no reason why I should try to convince you that, in my opinion, **'high school love' is the purest, most educational, most sweet, most fun love ever** (strictly my completely biased opinion). The important thing isn't always the journey, I always say, it's the lesson!

That said, I give you:

"Tsanonda's DIAMOND Rule Regarding Relationships"

(Please read and heed extremely carefully because this rule is the basis for every relationship that you or anyone you know will ever be a part of):

"THERE ARE NO RULES."

Yes, you read correctly, and I stand behind it 100%. The reality is there aren't any hard, fast rules that I, or anybody else, can give you that will magically make you or your mate/partner/potential partner have a successful relationship. What works for me or her or him may never work for you.

But, as with all things, there are guidelines that can help you make better choices which will make navigating the road to love less bumpy. So, based on the relationships I've been a part of and the women I've been involved with, here are some things I've learned and taken to heart:

-History with a person doesn't guarantee a successful relationship…

-Friendship with a person doesn't guarantee a successful relationship…

-Liking a person doesn't guarantee a successful relationship…

-LOVING a person doesn't guarantee a successful relationship…

Now, there are certain relationship staples, like strong communication, trust, thoughtfulness, honesty, loyalty, physical intimacy, common interests/goals and commitment to one another and the relationship, that are vital to beginning and maintaining a great relationship.

There really is, however, only one primary 'idea' I've learned that embodies the absolute backbone to an ideal, long lasting and mutually rewarding intimate relationship (or any relationship, honestly). That idea, ladies and gentlemen:

Reciprocal Sacrifice…

Follow me: People ramble on and on about compromise in relationships and that's good, but compromise is not enough. In these days and times where threesomes are the norm and polyamorous relationships (relationships involving multiple lifelong partners) are springing up, compromise is just a start.

If you want something enduring and worth every ounce of you, you have to be willing to give a little more than you usually would. You have to work harder and dig deeper than what was previously acceptable with anyone else. You have to take a step beyond compromise and consistently show you're willing to make sacrifices for the betterment of your relationship. Then, do that with someone who does the exact same for you.

Sacrifice (noun): Destruction or surrender of something for the sake of something or someone else…

Reciprocal (adjective): Given, felt, or done in return…

Reciprocal sacrifice…

Destroy your ego, along with old thoughts of how relationships should work, and surrender your heart and yourself for the sake of love eternal. Then, be blessed and patient enough to join with someone who will devote themselves to reciprocating that… Period.

Now on to an apology...

A reality of life is that apologies are extremely necessary. Not the reactionary kind you say as soon as you do something wrong then follow that "sorry" with a reason why you did it and then quickly offer even more reasons why the other person deserved whatever your action or hurtful words were anyway. Those types of apologies are pointless. They don't help the other person feel better, which, in my humble opinion, is one of the primary purposes of an apology. Besides, it makes you appear shallow.

I believe that apologies are like a mild salve, a home remedy, if you will: It's not as good as taking preventative measures (never doing or saying what you did or said), but it makes the person feel a little better instantly and initiates the healing process.

With that said, I apologize…

To any woman I've hurt, disrespected, emotionally or mentally scarred, pushed away or otherwise damaged in even the slightest way. Regardless of how 'unintentional' it was. **No excuses.**

I believe I've held the company of some of the most beautiful, intelligent, profound, dynamic women in the DMV. If I showed you these women's personal and professional resumes and invited them in a room together, they could probably solve many of humankinds' problems with relative ease. What stands out in my mind about each of them and sets them apart from others I've met is **the amount of heart and compassion they showed** to me, their friends, their families and others on the consistent basis, and it shows in most things they've created or are a part of currently.

The women I've spent time or titles with have, for the most part, been wonderful and I treasure their presence in my life, appreciate the time spent and value the lessons learned. And I offer a heartfelt apology. **No excuses.**

NOW ON to FRIENDSHIPS

Where to begin...

First and foremost, I'd like to say I have the absolute, hands down, no-point-in-attempting-to-develop-an-argument best friends in the world. The beauty of knowing this is I'm positive you can readily say the same thing about your friends, too.

And that's what makes friendships so great. It's like having the first five picks in a fantasy draft. It's unfair you actually get to choose these people! Now, while I could run down a list of people that I absolutely love, adore, appreciate and consider close friends, it would make this reminiscent of the 'Thank Yous' on the inside of an album cover (do artists still do that?). So, I must highlight a few of my closest friends and why these people have had an immensely profound and consistent impact on my life:

First, Mike, Brandon and Jamie...

My brothers... These three are my best friends since high school. We met each other early on and are still friends to this day. They had ringside seats to this continuous play called life, and each of them has taught me something different about life and been there for crucial parts of my development. Whether it was Brandon asking his father if I could stay with them after leaving my mother's house, or Mike telling me to stop letting people take advantage of me, or James telling me to check myself and my pride or all of them sharing their parents and families with me as I grew up with difficulties with my own. They've meant a lot to me individually and as a collective.

Now the specifics and I promise to keep it brief:

Michael Miller- Truly one of a kind… He's a master motivator. The difference between him and other motivators is he believes in your greatness and you find yourself being better than you are because you want him to be right. That's, Mike Miller…

Brandon Wylie- The younger sibling you figure you'll have to protect for the rest of your natural life, who starts speaking and acting and pushing and encouraging and supporting you like the big brother you always needed. That's B. Wylie…

James Crowder- Everyone needs a friend who knows how to listen. He's intelligent, gives good advice, and can tell you exactly what he thinks you should do. But instead, he allows you to pour yourself out without interruption or judgment. Those times when I feel like a sponge that has soaked up so much from work or people, I reach out to Jamie and he's always there to listen. That's, Jamie…

They're the brothers I chose, and I thank God for them daily. **Above It All**, I'm my brothers' maker… #MBJT #AboveItALL   #FirstFamily   #FamilyFirst #LoveLaughterAndLife

Now, on to my other life-defining friends in no particular order:

Tania White- One of my favorite lady friends! I can confide in her and be completely, utterly, laughably honest. She listens and responds with the honest truth. She doesn't pull punches and is considerate and hilarious, all at the same time. She's strong, intelligent, beautiful and one of my favorite people on the planet. Love you, Pookie.

Larry Saddler- My best friend from college. I met this guy in an English class, worked with him in the Office of Community Service, and we've been rolling tight ever since. His deposit into my being? Teaching me to shut up and stop being so subjective that I miss what's really going on around me. He taught me objectivity and perspective... Love you for that, Burner.

Terry McClellan- I amassed a large array of friends and associates in college (shouts to the McKeldin Crew!), but no one has been a rock (both physically and mentally) like this guy. He constantly reminds me to dream big, share my talents, and no matter how long it goes between conversations between us, it's always all good. Love you for that, "little" Bro.

Kori Richardson- He helps me stay grounded and is a constant reminder of my past: not the parts that made me hate myself and my life (although he was there for all of it), but the parts that made us laugh and never want to grow up. Those parts made us the great and still growing people we are today. Love you, Kori.

Michelle (Green) Evans- She is my ultimate cheerleader! We met at Morgan State after learning I had a cousin that started attending years after I arrived on campus. Always wanting a little sister, I called her immediately, we met the next day and the rest is history. What makes her so important to me? She tells me to forgive myself and acknowledge my greatness on the regular basis. Love you, Puppy.

Victorious Hall- This brother probably had no idea the mental struggles I battled before and after I returned to Morgan and met him. Vic made me realize that the coolest person I could possibly be was me… No hidden expectations. No agenda. No judgment. Trust me, he'd laugh at me when necessary, but it was always in love and light and with family (both blood and extended) at the core. He helped me build confidence in being authentically me. Love you for that, Vic.

Me'Shelle Shields- The wife of my mentor/favorite teacher, **Lamarr D. Shields** (who was quoted in the beginning of this book). Listen closely: This woman is EVERYTHING… She's a wife, a mom, a comedian. She's smart and engaging and humble. And occasionally, throughout my years of knowing her and her husband, she'll tell me, in so many words, that I'm worthy of greatness, but I must trust it, develop it, and allow it to shine. For that, and for marrying the man I love and model my life after, I appreciate and adore you and your husband, Queen.

Danee' Edwards– A peaceful WIFE... There's no compromise for it. This woman embodies it and passes her peace onto me. She's also taught me the real meaning of love, support and the value of family. For that and so much more, I love you, Pooh. And yes folks, even with different lives and loves in between, high school crushes can turn into happily ever after...

Gemius Edwards- My biological brother AKA Bro Ham! We've had our issues in the past, but he's the only person who has a first-person account of our life growing up. Having someone to go through your hell with is pretty cool when you think about it. Plus, he still treats me like his little brother and has never stopped holding me down to this day. Love you for that, Jimmy.

Kim Green- You blessed me with my son and are a living, breathing example of making co-parenting work. I could write a TON about our adventures, but I'll leave that for our book (Coming Soon!). I love and appreciate you, Doc.

Adia Jones and the ELLiS Crew- Adia and this group of kids (who are now adults doing AMAZING things individually) taught me that it's ok to love on a group of high schoolers that aren't your own and allow them to be themselves and grow into their greatness. They also taught me the meaning of unconditional love in the truest sense. Thank you, Adia and my sons and daughters (whichever one of you is reading this right now, YOU are my favorite!). I love you all.

And, there are others I have an extreme amount of love and appreciation for, but the aforementioned people have aided in shaping and molding me into the man I am today. I literally wouldn't be here without them...

So, why am I taking time and space to list people in my life for you?

My reasoning is simple: **identifying and acknowledging your support system is one of the most important projects you'll ever undertake.**

In fact, it's an ongoing process that you'll continue to perfect throughout your life as people enter and exit your personal and professional circle. One of the coolest things I hear on the regular basis is "Wow? You all are still friends?!" Yes. We are...

But there are also times when it can be heartbreaking when people you label 'friend' turn out to be cancers in your life. So, choose the friends you make family very carefully.

Takeaway from CHAPTER SIX

What's the singular most important relationship you can have?

The most important thing that you can do to create strong friendships, intimate relationships, or relationships of any kind is this:

Really, really get to know yourself…

It's as simple (and maybe as complicated) as that.

What I'm saying and have been saying (if you haven't noticed the pattern, yet) is understanding yourself is your most important undertaking. It goes well beyond whether you like books as opposed to movies or Italian food instead of Mexican or even what sexual orientation you identify as. As important as those factors are in your life, there are other details that seem small, but play a significant role in your interactions with others. For instance, you need to know if you're a talker or more of a listener. Then, know how comfortable you are around people who are the opposite of you or struggle to do the things you do well. Know if you like lots of human interaction or if you're ok spending time alone. Then, know how much and in what doses you want your friends and/or your mate to exhibit those qualities.

A firm understanding of who you are and your deeper likes and dislikes is the greatest step you can take toward forming lasting bonds with others. And this doesn't give you the right to be judgmental toward others because they're different from you. It just gives you the ability to prepare for the different personalities you'll contact or connect with. Even if those different personalities are your own…

ACTIVITY for CHAPTER SIX

Activity 1: Those 'Getting to Know Yourself' ideas in the TAKEAWAY section? Start writing...

There's nothing like having an actual tangible record of who you are. It's what makes having a diary or journal so incredible. You can even sit around with friends or your significant other and find out their perceptions of you while you give them your perceptions of them. One of the coolest things some of my friends have learned about me is I'm more of an introvert who has to cope with anxiety than the extrovert many see me as (I'm actually an 'ambivert'- having qualities of both extroverts and introverts). I had to learn that about myself and accept it. The point is, the more of an expert you are on yourself, the deeper your appreciation for you. And then for others...

Activity 2: Revisit that list that included the members of your support system a chapter back. Now, poll those folks. Survey your brothers, sisters, cousins, friends, parents, aunts, uncles, mentors, etc. Talk to them about how they view you: Ask them silly, 'surface-y' questions like what they think your favorite color is or your favorite cereal, just to see what their responses are and how much they know about you. Then ask them the deeper more intimate questions like what they think your gifts are or what they believe your purpose is. These are the questions that'll open your eyes

to what some of the most important people in your life see in you. This exercise will help propel you to another level of knowing yourself; an additional mirror from the perspective of those who truly care. It'll never take the place of knowing yourself, but it will allow you to see yourself through the eyes of others which can be helpful as you build a positive self-concept.

CHAPTER SEVEN

Our Next Steps

I hope that you were able to take something away from this book. It was cathartic to get some of these things out and while I know that all lives differ, I also know that we can learn from one another. My life was simply a backdrop to a few lessons known, reminded, or newly learned.

The reality is this: each day brings an opportunity to better your best or worst day. I'm living, breathing proof that you can face the odds and overcome them simply by tapping into the most valuable resource ever created: yourself.

Now where exactly do we go from here? You've read through the book and now (hopefully) feel a renewed sense of self; a realization of your personal trials and tribulations and a newfound appreciation for your own ability to push past them with resilience and faith. There's also this awareness and understanding that everybody goes through something at one time or another and not everybody is wired the same, so the healing process differs from person to person. So, with all that said, again **what's next?**

The great thing is that this ending is only the beginning...

Let's start with men...

My brothers, I urge you to hold yourselves to an ever-increasing level of accountability that ensures we're taking care of ourselves, honoring our women, raising our children and building our communities. We must walk the walk of Kings. We mustn't merely speak the standard; we must BE the standard... We have to face and conquer barriers that deter us from reaching our fullest potential. **That includes making our own mental health one of those barriers we aren't afraid to speak on and overcome.** I find, too often, we're either ashamed of or downplay significantly where we are mentally. Both are extremes we can ill afford. As with most things, balance is key: be resilient and be honest. This allows us to be the leaders we're created to be and set the bar for ourselves, our mates, our families, and our communities.

My sisters, I ask that you continue to be the strong, beautiful, courageous, nurturing, magical beings you've always been. Be the living embodiment of everything a Queen exudes- live as such, expect only what is acceptable and receive nothing less than what is sufficient for royalty. And that standard that we Kings must set for one another, our families, and our communities? Hold us to it and uphold us WITH it... Understand where and when we fall short and encourage us to stand up and be our best selves simply by reminding us of our heritage, our bloodlines, our greatness. Be the mirror that shows us that potential is good, but the expectation is now higher. The goal: **Transformative greatness.** And nothing short of it...

Young people, remember this rarely stated advice: **it's ok to be a follower...** That's why there is an actual being called a 'role model.' That sage advice comes with an increasingly important caveat: follow only when you're mimicking the example of those who have their and your absolute best interest at heart. How can you tell?

By following those that consistently show you their very best selves. The ones that are kind, respectful, thoughtful, considerate, creative, smart, have integrity, and are dedicated to everyone's success, not just their own.

Follow people who navigate the world in a way that spreads joy and peace and equity and strength and friendly laughter and light. Because that's excellence. That's leadership. Follow those kinds of people. Or accept your role as leader because who knows: that person just might be you...

And now that you understand how to only follow greatness, if in fact, you haven't reached your greatness threshold yet, what does that leave for you? **That leaves you to be the very best 'YOU' you can be...** No, you aren't expected to be perfect and you shouldn't feel pressure to do so. You are expected, however, to put in the work to polish your character: treat people fairly, be confident, be a good person, be a good teammate, set goals, achieve them, set new ones, WORK HARD, be humble, use your instincts, have integrity, LISTEN... All this simply means be the very best version of yourself you can possibly be because no one else can do that. Besides, every crew needs a 'you' in it! And that's the role you're perfectly made for...

And now, to **EVERYONE...**

There's literally one life to live.

One...

Don't live one day of it doubting your self-worth. We're all worthy of never ending amounts of joy and peace and fulfillment. But we must believe it if it is to be so...

So, go be great. Be wonderful. Be happy. But most, importantly, be EXTRAordinary...

Notes

Notes

Notes

Notes

Notes

Notes

Notes

Children's books and so much more

COMING SOON!

Please continue to follow my work and look for all
updates at www.TsanondaCares.com

For mental health services for youth and other youth and adult programs and workshops, please contact my team and I (**Above It All**) at www.aiahealth.org

"Be aware that you're rare…"

-Author Unknown, but obviously brilliant

#BEextraORDINARY